AN

ABC

OF

Gardening

SALLY MALTBY

KYLE CATHIE LIMITED

First published in Great Brita
in 1997 by
Kyle Cathie Limited,
20 Vauxhall Bridge Road,
London SW1V 2SA

ISBN 1 85626 269 3

A Cataloguing in Publication record for this title is available
from the British Library.

Reprographics by
Artwork Creative Services, Southampton

Printed in Singapore

& TO JENNY AND ALL AT
ARTWORK FOR INVALUABLE
TECHNICAL SUPPORT AND
ADVICE.

All thanks to
Caroline Taggart at
Kyle Cathie for among
other things letting
me get away - against
her better judgement
- with an Herbaceous
plant, and to Kyle
hoping that she has
changed her mind
about Borage...

A Gardening book for Robert, a ma
whose fingers remain unsoiled and
with whose help this project woulc
certainly never have got off the
ground.

The results of various successes & failures in my garden

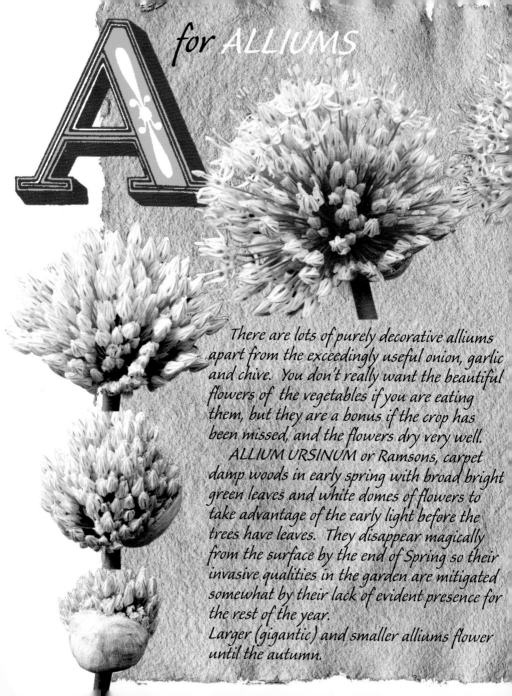

A for ALLIUMS

There are lots of purely decorative alliums apart from the exceedingly useful onion, garlic and chive. You don't really want the beautiful flowers of the vegetables if you are eating them, but they are a bonus if the crop has been missed, and the flowers dry very well.

ALLIUM URSINUM or Ramsons, carpet damp woods in early spring with broad bright green leaves and white domes of flowers to take advantage of the early light before the trees have leaves. They disappear magically from the surface by the end of Spring so their invasive qualities in the garden are mitigated somewhat by their lack of evident presence for the rest of the year.

Larger (gigantic) and smaller alliums flower until the autumn.

A could also be for ALLOTMENTS

Originally parcels of land were allocated for use by the 'labouring poor' as part of the Enclosures Act in England in 1845. Up to this time there had been a system of common land available.

More recently, in 1908, the Allotment Act placed an obligation on local councils to provide ~ if six ratepayers required it ~ small parcels of land for individuals to raise crops for their own consumption.

Allium aflatunense, albopilosum, beesianum, azureum, cyaneum, giganteum, moly, narcissiflorum, neopolitanum, oreophilum, rosenbachianum, schubertii, siculum, triquetrum....

Allotments in England still tend to be measured in square 'rods', 90 x 30 ft.
The relationship of square to linear rods seems obscure.
A linear rod is part of the archaic forms of measurement involving poles and perches ~ around 5 metres.
The size of a rod is related to the usable length of wood in the average tree, and the measurement of 16ft 6in or 5m, and modules of this, are used in traditional buildings.

BIRDS

Without which no garden would be complete; they lift the heart AND eat the pests – and – it must be admitted, sometimes the crops as well.

In winter when gardening tasks are temporarily over and the summer birds are gone, you can imitate the bird's song on an instrument of your choice.

A blackbird

BEGONIAS

A very diverse family with leaves of every type, size and pattern. The leaf lobes of some grow into single and double spirals. The ideal tolerant houseplants, there will be one of them in flower at any time of the year.

A Thrush

 *is for*

 ANTERBURY

ELLS

Canterbury Bells are one of two sorts of biennial Campanula ~
Campanula medium (Campanula pyramidalis is the other one).
As they flower in their second year of growth you have to be patient and
encourage the first year's rosette of leaves in order to have an amazing
spire of nursery~rhyme silver~blue bells in the second year, or silvery
cup~and~saucers if you have grown the Calycanthema species.

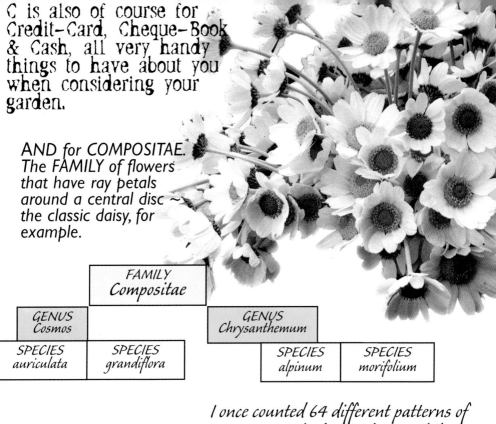

C is also of course for Credit-Card, Cheque-Book & Cash, all very handy things to have about you when considering your garden.

AND for COMPOSITAE. The FAMILY of flowers that have ray petals around a central disc ~ the classic daisy, for example.

FAMILY *Compositae*			
GENUS *Cosmos*		GENUS *Chrysanthemum*	
SPECIES *auriculata*	SPECIES *grandiflora*	SPECIES *alpinum*	SPECIES *morifolium*

I once counted 64 different patterns of CYCLAMEN leaf in and around the Alpine Houses at the Royal Horticultural Society's gardens at Wisley, England.

also CLEMATIS, especially the species and the ridiculously pretty florida alba plena & florida seiboldii.

IS FOR
DAHLIAS

Dahlias are wonderful
Dahlias are easy to grow
Dahlias smell amazing
Dahlia flowers can
be large & red or subtle
coloured, striped or anything
in between.

As to keeping dahlia tubers over winter – that's another matter. For years I've done the approved thing, keeping them in boxes, frost free and just damp, with limited success. I do, though, have two plants in the garden that have resisted frosts and appear again from year to year – maybe some kind of answer to the keeping problem is to plant them deep, out of the way of at least medium-strength frosts.

I have a collection of striped DIANTHUS, too.

ear-wigs sometimes live in dahlias

eCcentricity

EGO

ExCess

exhibition

Eccentricity in gardens can be directed towards the architecture, but there are some pretty eccentric plants as well, particularly ones adapted to very special conditions, and others created by human intervention, such as the appalling double antirrhinum and the red delphinium. But the passionate pursuit of an IDEA is what makes some gardens so interesting.

One of the most eccentric gardens I know is the garden at Bomarzo near Rome. It is full of extraordinary gigantic archetypal figures, carved from the existing rocky out-crops and surrounded by a 'sacred wood'. Vicino Orsini created an entirely enigmatic and personal garden which astounds the visitor and confounds convention.

apple tree, it's important to go along with your ideas at whatever scale is appropriate to your circumstances. If it seems like a good idea to uproot the roses and plant for one glorious monocultural display, or to create a World of Disney in your own small patch, then do it.

So, whether it's the ideal palace or the ideal gnome, the ideal herbaceous border or the ideal collection of plants that particularly interests you, whether you have an ambition to grow the largest pumpkin in the world or perhaps to own an

FORCE

and
fritillaries

which does actually seem rather
a misnomer, encouragement might be
more appropriate

What is going on here is
an encouragement of the life-force, and need
for plants to grow up.
Various vessels have been evolved for this purpose,
not only to give protection in order to harvest earlier
crops, but generally to exclude light so that the
blanched shoots of rhubarb and sea-kale will be

tender and sweet.

How to force chicory.

Sow seeds in late spring, thin the germinated ones to around 20cm or 8in apart and weed the plants as necessary. Then spend some of the summer searching for appropriate cardboard boxes ~ another useful accessory would be cardboard tubes which you can gather at your convenience. These could be put over the crowns to encourage tight growth. The boxes should probably be rectangular and require a top ~ another box, perhaps ~ the main boxes have to accommodate a depth of soil, the root and the consequent shoot, so should be at least 40cm or 16in deep. Plastic boxes could be used but are somehow not quite so versatile; a dark cellar or shed might also be suitable. The advantage of the cardboard boxes however, is that while they are portable you also have the moral satisfaction of re-using something.

*In late autumn dig up the large leafy plants, cut off the leaves to around 2.5cm or 1in above the crown, and trim the side roots to the long tap root (which **can** be used as an adulterant for coffee). The rather coarse leaves could be chopped and used in salad, made into a nutritious soup, or, no doubt, cooked as spinach.*

Pack the roots closely together in the boxes and fill with fine soil or sand which should be just damp. Cover to exclude light and, depending on the temperature, ideally around 10°C or 55°F, shoots will be ready for cutting at about 15cm or 6in long in between 3 to 6 weeks. The roots will be depleted by their premature growth, so after shooting abandon them to the compost heap or they might rot.

GRAVEL
provides a maintenance~free (well, almost) substrate which discourages weeds, makes a permanent mulch and water~retaining surface on the soil and allows you to plant where you will. Its biggest disadvantage is that you cannot, without some trouble, put compost on it, as you would to enrich bare soil, but, in order not to have to deal with a lawn-mower ~ I'll take the trouble.

For *GRASS*	**Against** *GRASS*
1. *Covers a large area with bland green.*	1. *It is very bland, but there are advantages if you have considerable acres to deal with.*
2. *Soft to walk on.*	2. *Muddy.*
3. *Good for children and croquet.*	3. *Children probably prefer the local rec. ~ I concede the argument when it comes to croquet.*
4. *You can lie on it.*	4. *A nice chair ensures that you don't share yourself with ants and other predatory insects.*
5. *It grows nice things like daisies and moss.*	5. *The whole idea of a lawn is that you are meant to kill the daisies and the moss.*

But the main reason against grass is that you have to buy a lawn~mower; most days in the summer you spend a long time starting and maintaining the thing, and cutting your carefully grown grass to the ground.

Zonal GERANIUMS
are generally, and wrongly, referred
to as Geraniums; they should really be
called Zonal Pelargoniums, and the hardy
herbaceous perennials called Geraniums.
They both rightly belong to the Geraniaceae
family.   However, common
usage has in this case
put paid to
nomenclaturial
tyranny and we
carry happily on
calling Zonal
Pelargoniums
collectively ~ but
wrongly ~ Geraniums,
on those occasions when
exact differentiations
are not required.

H

An Herbaceous plant, i.e. one that retreats into the ground after flowering and does not make persistent woody growth, obviously has a relationship to a Herb (why not <u>an</u> Herb?). 'Herbs' have come rather loosely to refer to plants with a medicinal or culinary use, but there are non-Herbaceous Herbs: rosemary, lavender, sage and thyme all do make persistent growth. I wonder what would happen to an Herbaceous plant in a consistent climate – would it die down or keep growing?

is for HOSTA.
You probably want your hostas to look like
this, or this, or this,
but because of this they might
quite well look like this.

for
IRIS

he Iris flowers differ in structure from those of other plants. Three outer
tals hang down and are called 'falls', the other three stand up and are
own as 'standards'. There are also three 'stylus' in the centre which
semble and are coloured as the standards.

is can be in bloom for most of the year from the early Iris stylosa to Iris
ata in late Autumn; an Iris will grow in most situations from a soggy
g to a sun~drenched gravel bed. The most familiar bearded and beardless
izomous Iris flower in early Summer.

It's a red Iris shown on the coat of arms of the City
of Florence in Italy ~ not Prince of Wales feathers.
There has been a long~running competition to breed a
real red Iris in Italy and the results can be seen above
the river Arno, below the church of San Miniato in the
florentine Iris Garden.
At their best in May the results of the quest are
magnificently displayed ~ mainly, it has to be said, so far,
in varying shades of brown, but nonetheless beautiful.
But here also are all the glorious blues of a Virgin's dress
and every shade and shape of frilly lingerie~inspired Iris
that you could wish to see...

J for

Juniper are conifers, but are one of the rare ones that will grow happily in dry alkaline soil. Maybe because of this the colour of junipers tends to be a softer and less uniform green than that of most conifers and it therefore doesn't look foreign in alkaline gardens.

JUNIPER

& FOR JIN
FLAVOURED WITH
JUNIPER

There are numerous varieties of Juniper, both horizontal and vertical, and generally dense growing. In northern gardens Juniper communis 'Hibernica' will probably be as near as you can get to the admired pencil cypresses of warmer climates (a cypress, Cupressus sempervirens).

Juniper varieties show
two different sorts of leaf, the juvenile or thin spiky leaf, and the
mature or scale~like leaf.   Some juniper, such as Juniper virginiana
(confusingly known as the Pencil Cedar) show both sorts of leaf.

after a hard day being jaunty in the 'jardin' the jaded,
but jubilant and jovial journeyman judges it judicious and
justifiable at this juncture to drink a jigger of jin
— and juice...

Gardening is an attempt to control and synthesise
rampant surrounding Nature, and along the way to
create a private Arcadia where all is well and balanced
and fruitful.

is for KNOT

KNOT GARDENS ARE REAL CONTROLLERS'
GARDENS AS THE BOX — AND IT USUALLY IS
BOX, BEING AN AMENABLE, DENSE-GROWING
PLANT — HAS TO BE MINUTELY SHAPED AND
DESIGNED TO MAKE THE TOP LINES OF THE
BUSHES APPARENTLY GO UNDER AND OVER
THEMSELVES IN CELTIC CONVOLUTIONS.

I first saw decorative KALE planted out in rows in Marie Antoinette's recreational village, Le Petit Hameau, in the grounds of Versailles (France). They seemed wonderfully appropriate, a play vegetable for a play farm.

Ivy

Heuchera

Begonia

Heuchera

Aquilegia

Begonia Rex

Anemone Japonica

for LEAVES

Ipomoea

Pelargoni

CO_2

Hypoestes

sugars
for
growth

O_2

H_2O

Begonia

Comfrey

Ivy

Cornus

Geranium

Geranium

Peperomia

Coleus

Not only beautiful but very, very important as, by the interchange of oxygen and carbon dioxide in photosynthesis, they make the very air we breathe.

Primrose

Caladium

Passion Flower

Maidenhair Fern

Abutilon

Alchemilla

Diffenbachia

MUD

Two of the classical elements of EARTH
and WATER mixed, but still a nuisance.
It can of course be combined with FIRE,
in the presence of AIR
to make flower pots for the garden . . . . . .

The real problem as far as most plants are concerned
is that mud excludes AIR and walking on wet ground
compacts soil particles and - excludes AIR.
The roots of most plants cannot function without air
and compaction also hinders the progress of the
all-important earth-worms that mix organic matter
into the soil and improve drainage at the same time.

A really useful thing to do with mud is to mix it with
seed and spray it into inaccessible or difficult
growing places, like motorway banks or cliffs.

M IS ALSO FOR MEDLAR

*An exceptionally pretty
Renaissance sort of a tree
with ethereal flowers in the
Spring, large bright green
leaves throughout the
growing year and the bonus
of unusual and intriguing
hip-like fruit that will not
be edible until rotten,
or mud-coloured.*

THE TREE IS ALSO ATTRACTIVE, I FIND TO MY COST, TO COWS.

N *is for Nineteenth Century*

When vegetables grew in straight lines and the garden was full of magnificent flowers with which to adorn the house. The newly imported plants hadn't yet had time to grow to their full height and inconvenience. Things were largely organic as the noxious chemicals designed to assail the pests had not yet been invented, and there were plenty of horses around.

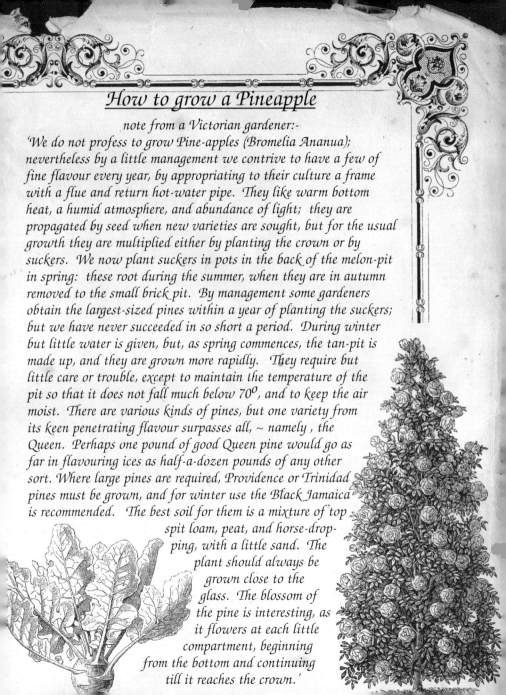

How to grow a Pineapple

note from a Victorian gardener:-

'We do not profess to grow Pine-apples (Bromelia Ananua); nevertheless by a little management we contrive to have a few of fine flavour every year, by appropriating to their culture a frame with a flue and return hot-water pipe. They like warm bottom heat, a humid atmosphere, and abundance of light; they are propagated by seed when new varieties are sought, but for the usual growth they are multiplied either by planting the crown or by suckers. We now plant suckers in pots in the back of the melon-pit in spring: these root during the summer, when they are in autumn removed to the small brick pit. By management some gardeners obtain the largest-sized pines within a year of planting the suckers; but we have never succeeded in so short a period. During winter but little water is given, but, as spring commences, the tan-pit is made up, and they are grown more rapidly. They require but little care or trouble, except to maintain the temperature of the pit so that it does not fall much below 70°, and to keep the air moist. There are various kinds of pines, but one variety from its keen penetrating flavour surpasses all, ~ namely , the Queen. Perhaps one pound of good Queen pine would go as far in flavouring ices as half-a-dozen pounds of any other sort. Where large pines are required, Providence or Trinidad pines must be grown, and for winter use the Black Jamaica is recommended. The best soil for them is a mixture of top spit loam, peat, and horse-dropping, with a little sand. The plant should always be grown close to the glass. The blossom of the pine is interesting, as it flowers at each little compartment, beginning from the bottom and continuing till it reaches the crown.'

...for Orchards, where you recline
in your deckchair with a book on
a clement afternoon protected
from the need to do anything by
the relentless forces of Nature
hard at work around you. The
seasons pursue their natural
course from spring to summer to
harvest, and the trees, attended by
a balance of malevolent and
benevolent animals and insects, mark
the seasons with almost imperceptible
but inevitable change.

FROM A NINETEENTH-CENTURY
GARDENING BOOK:-

"OF ALL OUR FRUITS, THE APPLE IS PERHAPS THE
MOST USEFUL, AND IS APPRECIATED BY BIRDS AND
BEASTS AS WELL AS BY MAN. MY BULLFINCH
LOVES HIS SLICE OF APPLE, MY HORSE THANKS ME
BY MANY LITTLE SIGNS FOR THE GIFT OF AN
APPLE AND MY COWS DELIGHT TO BE OFFERED
ONE. THE PIGS, THE CHICKENS, THE GEESE, ALL
RUN TO SEIZE THE WINDFALLS AS THEY DROP,
AND SOMETIMES THE CHICKENS GET INTO THE
TREES TO PROCURE THE FRUIT......MY COLLECTION
OF APPLES COMPRISES NEARLY THREE HUNDRED
VARIETIES. IT IS NEITHER ADVISABLE NOR
EXPEDIENT HOWEVER, TO HAVE SO MANY KINDS..."

for ponds

Sand-strewn caverns, cool and deep
Where the winds are all asleep;
Where the spent lights quiver and gleam;
Where the salt weed sways in the stream;
Where the sea-beasts rang'd all round
Feed in the ooze of their pasture-ground...
Where great whales come sailing by,
Sail and sail with unshut eye,
Round the world for ever and aye.

Matthew Arnold
The Forsaken Merman

Ponds, however small, lend an enigmatic air to part of the garden. Their inhabitants live in a foreign element and lead mysterious lives.

Q is for quotes from an English Victorian Garden.

Truffle hunting.

'The truffle is found abundantly at the "Oaks" in the next parish. It is a fungus which grows underground under the shade of certain kinds of trees, preference being given to the beech tree. It likes a stratum of loam lying over chalk.

It is found by persons who specially devote their time to this object. There are but few truffle-hunters in this country; nevertheless I found one after some trouble and persuaded him to take me out for a day's hunt. He had an active little dog, that was trained to find the truffle by scent ~ a bit of cheese was given to it whenever it found one. To train the dog at first a truffle was placed in an old shoe and its food depended on it finding out where it was.....In two or three hours we found about three pounds in weight....The Morel grows in my garden, especially under large elm-trees. In some years we have had great abundance and in most years we have some.'

Elm trees.

'First and foremost, there are gigantic English Elms of many centuries growth, in the upper branches of which rooks delight to build, and under their shade the cattle protect themselves from the mid~day sun.....It is not much planted at the present time round London as of late years it has extensively died, and in our London parks has been replaced by the plane~tree.'

Rowan trees.

'In Scotland it is one of the greatest ornaments of the mountains; but in my garden it has not, up to the present time, been of any importance. Formerly the rowan-tree was an object of superstition. The berries used to be tied round the necks of children to preserve them from witchcraft.....From inquiries I made in Scotland this year, it appears that this superstition no longer exists, and a forester, in answer to my interrogations, declared that "the schoolmaster had driven it away". A similar superstition exists to this day at Naples, where people of education and position use charms of red coral for a similar purpose.'

Box trees.

'We use it for edging the walks, as it bears any amount of clipping. Our forefathers used to cut the tree into the form of birds or animals, which occasionally may be seen in country villages. The best example of clipped trees I ever saw was at the Pope's garden attached to the Vatican in Rome, where amongst other animals a cow with its horns is marvellously rendered by clipping a tree. This horticultural extravagance, though not to be admired, is interesting, as showing the extent to which some trees may be clipped and deformed by ill-bestowed patience and care.'

Pumpkins.

'We grow Pumpkins rather more for the pleasure of seeing them than for their intrinsic value. They are used in apple~pies, but the pies are better with apples alone ~ without the pumpkins....'

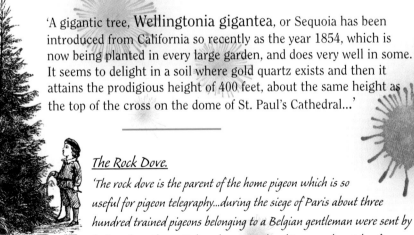

Wellingtonia gigantea.

'A gigantic tree, **Wellingtonia gigantea,** or Sequoia has been introduced from California so recently as the year 1854, which is now being planted in every large garden, and does very well in some. It seems to delight in a soil where gold quartz exists and then it attains the prodigious height of 400 feet, about the same height as the top of the cross on the dome of St. Paul's Cathedral...'

The Rock Dove.

'The rock dove is the parent of the home pigeon which is so useful for pigeon telegraphy...during the siege of Paris about three hundred trained pigeons belonging to a Belgian gentleman were sent by balloon from the capital, and were employed to carry despatches from thence. The messages were set up in type and photographed on collodion, so minutely that they could not be deciphered by the unaided eye.... These aerial messengers baffled the military skill of the Germans who in their turn employed hawks to kill the pigeons, but, it is believed, with little or no success.'

ROSES

There are few gardening experiences quite so awe-inspiring as the first flowering of ROSES. If the weather has been fine then 'Souvenir de Malmaison' will open its full quartered glory to the sun. The massive flowers of 'Madame Isaac Pereire' will age from the initial startling shocking-pink to a more subtle purple-pink. 'Fruhlingsgold' will probably have nearly finished its great swathes of yellow double rosettes.

As the flower of roses in the spring of the year, as lilies by the rivers of water, and as the branches of the frankincense tree in the time of summer

Ecclesiasticus ch.50.v.8.

The vast pink bowls of 'Constance Spry' will shine out in the evening; 'La Reine Victoria' and 'Pierre Oger' will have defied black-spot and be laden with delicate globes of petals; 'Great Maiden's Blush' sounds for all the world like a civilised eighteenth-century oath ('Cuisse de Nymph' is its French name describing the colour - presumably - of the thighs of a particular nymph). Another plant with expansionist ambitions, it will start on a long succession of flowering starting with buds that are the classic model for a rose-bud, with feathered calyx.

And so on through a sumptuous litany of names ...

'Baron Girod de l'Ain', & 'Cardinal de Richelieu' & 'Tricolour de Flandres' & 'Camaieux' & 'New Dawn' & 'Fantin-Latour' & 'Kiftsgate'& 'Nevada' & 'Félicité et Perpétue' & 'Ferdinand Pichard' & 'Ispahan' & 'Georges Vibert' & 'Comte de Chambord' & 'Reines des Violettes' & 'Roseraie de L'Hay' & & &

'Variegata di Bologna' will amaze again with Italian ice-cream stripes. If you pick the flowers early and store them in silica gel for some time you will have pretty dried buttons. 'Charles de Mille' is spreading at an alarming rate throughout the garden, but forgiven its ambitions for its deep claret flowers. 'New' roses, such as 'Heritage' and 'National Trust', are so heavy with flowers that they bend to almost touch the pond. The best way to see them is to study the reflections in the water disturbed only temporarily by the passage of a fish.

FOR SUNFLOWER

and the self~
congratulatory
'Wow, did I grow
that?' factor,
an Exhibition of
Vegetable
Exuberance.

& SQUASH

and SUMMER-TIME

is for

TREE

Trees are among the longest living
organisms on the planet and essential for
the immediate and long-term health of
everything.

A real compensation in winter
is the shapes of the deciduous trees, showing
their individual structures modified by
chance and weather.

URNS, traditionally the containers of funerary ashes and a suitable introduction into eighteenth-century gardens. They would strike just the right note of PENSIVE REFLECTION with HISTORICAL ASSOCIATIONS and bring an atmosphere of the PICTURESQUE AND SUBLIME to the garden... Then somebody realised how handy it would be to plant them up with flowers....

FOR
URNS

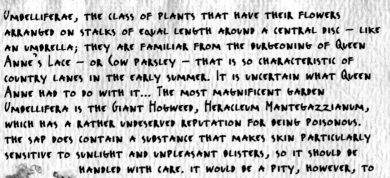

UMBELLIFERAE, THE CLASS OF PLANTS THAT HAVE THEIR FLOWERS ARRANGED ON STALKS OF EQUAL LENGTH AROUND A CENTRAL DISC — LIKE AN UMBRELLA; THEY ARE FAMILIAR FROM THE BURGEONING OF QUEEN ANNE'S LACE — OR COW PARSLEY — THAT IS SO CHARACTERISTIC OF COUNTRY LANES IN THE EARLY SUMMER. IT IS UNCERTAIN WHAT QUEEN ANNE HAD TO DO WITH IT... THE MOST MAGNIFICENT GARDEN UMBELLIFERA IS THE GIANT HOGWEED, HERACLEUM MANTEGAZZIANUM, WHICH HAS A RATHER UNDESERVED REPUTATION FOR BEING POISONOUS. THE SAP DOES CONTAIN A SUBSTANCE THAT MAKES SKIN PARTICULARLY SENSITIVE TO SUNLIGHT AND UNPLEASANT BLISTERS, SO IT SHOULD BE HANDLED WITH CARE. IT WOULD BE A PITY, HOWEVER, TO BAN THIS MAGNIFICENT PLANT FROM THE GARDEN UNLESS SKIN CONTACT IS REALLY UNAVOIDABLE OR IT IS NEAR WHERE CHILDREN ARE LIKELY TO PLAY.

B. UMBELLIFERAE

and VARIEGATED.
Variegation is often a very
desirable trait, the patterns and
colours of variegated leaves are
very intriguing. It may be
surprising that it is caused either
by a virus or by a genetic fault in
the developing cell ~ which is
responsible particularly for
lines of variegation.
Viruses tend to affect
younger leaves, and will of
course weaken the plant so
that it will be nothing like
as vigorous as the non-
variegated type. One
reason for this is that
the area available
for photosynthesis
is restricted
through lack of
chlorophyll.
These plants
should be grown
in good, but not
excessively
bright light,
which might
scorch them.

For
Violas, the
family that
includes
both Pansies
and Violets.
Pansies have
rounded petals,
Violets strap-
shaped ones.

There are so
many and various
sorts of *VIBURNUM*
that they would be
ideal for any situation.
They are small trees or
shrubs which generally have
white flowers arranged in clusters.
Flower shapes can vary from flat to spherical
and many of them have wonderful scent. Viburnum tinus *and*
V. grandifolia *cheer up the winter as they flower on bare wood all through the
season.* V. plicatum *or* tomentosum *has horizontal tiers of branches, bearing
large and flat-faced groups of flowers. The evergreen* V. x burkwoodi *is an ideal
hedge plant in a reasonably large space and although its main crop of flowers is
in spring, it also flowers for a good part of the winter. Then there is* V. opulus,
*the Guelder Rose, an indigenous tree, and much the most sophisticated of them
all, with splendid lipstick-red berries in the autumn. The other indigenous
species is the beautifully scented* V. lanata, *the Wayfaring-tree. As the berries
change from green to red to black as they ripen in autumn, you sometimes see
all three colours within the same bunch.*

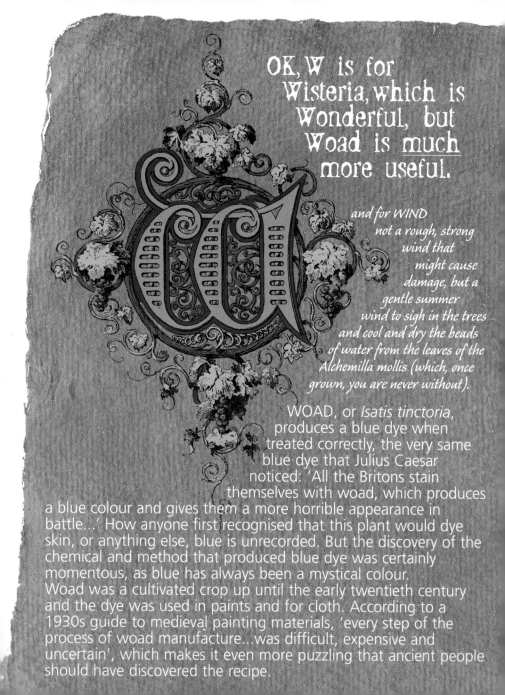

OK, W is for Wisteria, which is Wonderful, but Woad is <u>much</u> more useful.

and for WIND
not a rough, strong
wind that
might cause
damage, but a
gentle summer
wind to sigh in the trees
and cool and dry the beads
of water from the leaves of the
Alchemilla mollis (which, once
grown, you are never without).

WOAD, or *Isatis tinctoria*, produces a blue dye when treated correctly, the very same blue dye that Julius Caesar noticed: 'All the Britons stain themselves with woad, which produces a blue colour and gives them a more horrible appearance in battle...' How anyone first recognised that this plant would dye skin, or anything else, blue is unrecorded. But the discovery of the chemical and method that produced blue dye was certainly momentous, as blue has always been a mystical colour. Woad was a cultivated crop up until the early twentieth century and the dye was used in paints and for cloth. According to a 1930s guide to medieval painting materials, 'every step of the process of woad manufacture...was difficult, expensive and uncertain', which makes it even more puzzling that ancient people should have discovered the recipe.

The leaves of woad are traditionally stored dry and formed into balls which could be fermented, when needed, with water and treated with various chemicals to make a fast, strong dye ~ a notoriously smelly process involving thick fetid fumes.
If you grow woad ~ and it grows very easily ~ you can make some dye using this recipe and without the most of the fumes

HOW TO DYE WOOL USING YOUNG WOAD LEAVES

Take enough young fresh woad leaves to fill a heat~resistant jar with a screw top. Press the leaves down tightly in the jar, cover with just boiling water and continue filling the jar with leaves until the water overflows. Then screw on the top to exclude air. Maintain a heat of around 50°C or 120°F for about 10 hours to encourage fermentation. When you see bubbles from the fermentation, add a few tablespoons of liquid ammonia to the brew and stir until the liquid turns from yellow to green. Put clean, wet wool into the jar and top it up as previously, to exclude air. Allow the wool to steep for about an hour. Lift it out and it will turn pale blue in contact with air. Steep for a further half an hour, then expose the wool to the air again. You can carry on like this until you achieve the colour you want, or until the dye bath loses its strength. The dye can be reactivated by adding about 2 teaspoons of lime and a large pinch of bran.

for XENOLITH
from geology, a rock
or stone occurring in
a system to which is
does not belong.

OED

X can also mark the spot where a precious
plant will ~ or won't ~ emerge from a
difficult winter.

Many gardens have an exhibition of xenoliths gathered on walks along the sea, or other places where a particularly attractive pebble has been irresistible. It's a pity, though, that too many rockeries are made from specially imported stone, such as limestone paving. It not only tends to look wrong in the context ~ local stone should be used wherever possible ~ but causes irreparable harm to the natural landscape. Xenophobia should be encouraged in this case.

FOR *New*

As a dense and slow-growing plant yew is ideal for large topiary. It will also regenerate and sprout leaves from bare stems if trimmed right back.

Many churchyards have enormous ancient Yews. There have been lots of theories as to why they were planted ~ keeping animals from the churchyard, use of the wood for bows, etc. etc. The fact is that Yew tends to lose heart wood and go hollow after about 400 years, so it is impossible to verify their great age using the growth ring test. Other evidence suggests that some Yews are at least 2000 years old, which would give them an added pre-Christian sacred significance.

Z

A COLLECTION OF
PLANTS THAT DO NOT
LIKE THE COLD.

ZEBRINA
the easiest plant in the world to grow.

ZINNIA
wonderful colours,
subtle though bright.

ZANTEDESCHIA
aethiopica (the familiar
arum lily) and its relative
Zantedeschia elliottiana,
with spotted leaves.

How Auspicious to be able to
end an Abecedarian with a
cornucopia of strange plants
beginning with Z and to contrast
the Archetypical invincible Zebrinas
with an Amalgam of Agreeable and
Artless if only too weather sensitive
Zinnias and the Arcane spathes
of Arum Zantedeschia.

If you need to know more about any of the plants mentioned here, Kyle Cathie publishes three authoritative books:-

Jekka McVicar ~ Complete Herb Book
Bob Flowerdew ~ Complete Fruit Book
Matthew Biggs ~ Complete Book of Vegetables

Other references I find invaluable are:-
Reader's Digest Encyclopaedia of Garden Plants & Flowers
Hugh Johnson ~ The Principles of Gardening (Mitchell Beazley)
Christopher Lloyd ~ The Well-Tempered Garden (Penguin)
Graham Stuart Thomas ~ The Rock Garden and its Plants (J.M.Dent)